The Snow Globe

The Snow Globe

Jenny Pagdin

Nine
Arches
Press

The Snow Globe
Jenny Pagdin

ISBN: 978-1-913437-86-2
eISBN: 978-1-913437-87-9

First published February 2024 by:

Nine Arches Press
Unit 14, Sir Frank Whittle Business Centre,
Great Central Way, Rugby.
CV21 3XH
United Kingdom

www.ninearchespress.com

Printed on recycled paper in the United Kingdom by: Imprint Digital.

Nine Arches Press is supported using public funding by Arts Council England.

Supported using public funding by
**ARTS COUNCIL
ENGLAND**

For Nicholas, who held us when we were falling

Contents

Definition of love

Old English, related to leave and lief

Verbal noun: something known by its actions
(as the wind is); *noun:* nothing (in a contest);
the press of breath against a diver's chest
(symptoms include insomnia, digestive tension);
the invisible movement of lips on
lips forgetting to breathe. *Verb trans:* to be possessed
beyond all reason: not by one as he really exists
but he as if remade by your devotion.
Verb intrans: to be one with the birds in flight
and one with the deer that skit across the forest floor;
to touch skin along warm skin and make no break
unless he turns in sleep (*cf.* bulbs at night
that gleam in the darkened greenhouse, warm and sure;
nubbed roots which intertwine in earth). *Antonym:* heartache.

Family planning (i)

Pregnancy test

my voice
telling your Daddy
high as a zeppelin

_____

_____

your faint shadow
setting   sail at
the tiny porthole

_____

_____

our three lives
turned in a kaleidoscope
shaken and shaken
until they fall

Night crossing (i)

Labour

And when she took away the gas & air I didn't
know how I'd get across to the next one,
heavy, pressed bare against the rails, my hand
still grasping for the mask. I never cried
until she stitched me up – *it's like a jigsaw.*
You beached upon my chest – *latching.*

'Boy of Jenny Pagdin'

Navel clamped like a sandwich bag
forehead wax-red
wild arms stir the air. Branches.

Newborn

A paper jewellery box lined with kapok –
bolstering a seed and a light blue eggshell.
Then your name, that birthright that flew to
my chest like hail, bringing the male beauty
of winter. We used to whisper it through the
walls. You rooted around for my third gift
before it was offered, the rich hind-milk let
down. We nestled in. My body was yours.
We brought you lambs' wool with a memory
of snow, the softest corduroy, felt, muslin,
papooses and clockwork. Our flat filled up
with a flock of cards; the trees touched
foreheads where they met above the houses.

Gore

All our mothers have to buy us a cow's eye,
the polythene bags inside the paper ones.
Our scalpels slip hungrily, barely snagging,
on the sclera, choroid, retina. It surprises me
the toughness of optic nerves twisted in lilac,
the vitreous, like an amniotic sac,
and how quietly it is that twenty-eight hearts
can go on beating under crested sweaters
despite, despite.

~

When the Bounty photographer
asks me to dab the blood off you, I hate her.
That blood means the hours they made me push you,
inwardly whispering *get out,*
that blood means the hours of the hospital door
flipping death and life, it means my grandmother's voice,
it means latexed hands lifting you clear of me
and I, who capitulate at every turn,
am suddenly naked and defiant as my son
and I just will not, will not clean it.

Under the milk trance

Under the milk trance   the muslins and posset,
under the curds and whey   where cockleshells
    gleam bone   in a navy-blue garden
    and his creamed mouth tumbling from the breast
painless butterfly stitches   closing me
    till morning   clouds the milk-jar
his call lifting me   the nipple knotting
    in time with his rising cry   the leap of the tides
    to the moon-face   and may we all prevail.

Ma Lightkeeper's prayer

Oh Lord when a ship's lantern steers close
and my heart is in my mouth
guide this house through dangerous tides
keep us safe if he might fail to thrive
may the milky balm of light
pour across the troubled surface
of stark dreams, nourishing
and on these disheveled nights
the drowning seafarers

salt in their nostrils cries in the waves,
water in their mouths sheets in a knot
and should one body slip away
drifting full and bloated against the porthole
let me steer him back
back to the cot before the striped flashes
the next flare
Lord may we wake
milk-drunk and satiated and all unscathed.

Heavenly

A lilac evening years ago.
The dusk was doing that cocktail-of-pastels thing.

Mars came out, and Venus
and I wanted them to touch;

they soon had me in an institution, eddying
till the planet turned under its tape of stars

and to this day I can get jittery
because the sky just goes on and on

overcast, the tousled strands unwinding,
raw wool —

On Whom the Rain Comes Down

Title from Thomas Hardy's 'An Autumn Rain-Scene'

People do say never to touch a tent
that's heavy with water;
I barely even knew a woman could
get ill and hurt her child.

They said our baby had a higher risk,
for six months the odds were penciled on the wardrobe
while my auntie, cousins, friends,
succumbed to cancers, fraud or death.

They said our baby might have infantile hypotonia,
then he fainted and wouldn't come round,
I was sick and fainted and was sick, sick, sick
and still it rained down, crosshatching the sky.

Woolgathering

February

Outside the cinema
holding hands in our Smitten
my coat buttoned only once.
It's showing. I'm showing.

Learning granny squares
to calm my hands down,
to make this winter bearable.

April

Intricate woodland holds the dusk
amber and sapphire
over pared-back fields;
fleece twists in the barbed wire.

Slipping along the jetty
on evening walks
you steer me out of my thoughts.

May

They have dragged me, cindered,
down from a pyre.
The cot adjoins my bed.
I watch as my hands learn swaddling.

When the midwife comes
I snap *it's not that I can't dress him,*
it's just that all this knitting fumbles.

November

The other mothers' inflections
intrude on my dreams
yet they ignore my faltering speech,
voices bright and glassy.

Like living behind a screen,
gloved hands at the ATM,
trees disconnected in the fog.

What the weather plans to do

the weather plans to eat through
your bunting, to charcoal the sky,
to scurry your children indoors,
drive swans down onto the tracks.
It wants to rock the ferry
and blow the eggs hollow, fill
the empty shells with dank
greenbrown, dry the bladderwrack
round the fishing crates, lift out
the thoughts from your clean mind

Insanity

My mind blew open so wide, I couldn't trust the sun to set

Not tawny, never brass

First the sulphur of The Works in her nostrils
then brazening her way into a pick-up joint –
one gold stocking slouched below her skirt;

first a sweater in custard cashmere
then hair twisted under an oil-cloth sou'wester,
careering downhill in her Marigolds;

first pollen dabbed on each eyelid
then the reeling amber of hazard lights
and then a circle of worried faces;

first just a lemon tang in the mouth
then nudging mustard onto an isolated yolk
in the hospital occy-health kitchen.

Ursa Major

I wanted a deckchair on our roof for stargazing and though
we don't have a garden the roof is flat and I remember
rotating fluorescent star-charts above my head, aged
ten, but they were mapped for the wrong hemisphere so
I never learnt the constellations until over bacon sandwiches
an ex-boyfriend showed me the Plough in his parents' garden
and on the evening I put all the knives in the toaster,
and they sectioned me, I felt like I was in handcuffs
and I prefer doors now because then I was always going for
the window, pulling on the plastic handle like I couldn't
work it and roaring my lion's roar and the police were in
our bedroom, the neighbours at the door with deckchairs,
and James' little voice below and Orion's belt re-forming in
the Velux, and the policewoman saying he was fine he was
having his tea and between my coarse screams a rubber
black bar over me in the ambulance like the Big Dipper
and the paramedics' insinuations and the hospital guards
weeing on the floor of A&E and pushing my head back into
a seizure and planning to rape me, the one with the spangled
arms and the one who was super tall in that room which
moved like a lift and sometimes now I feel the full moon
zing like a ten-pee piece on my tongue, and I wheel my bike
through, and shrug, running through my constellations like a
tarot, my finger grazing on each star, trying to make them fit.

What to pack for the Caldbeck Mother & Baby Unit

- at least one floaty evening dress
- Bach remedies in a floral case
- an empty purse for emergencies
- cheese, for parties
- a magic book that reads itself
- your true colours, and a heart to wear pinned to the outside of your sleeve
- a pair of slippers
- a list of false names, for your child.

Night crossing (ii)

Insomnia

Making the terrible crossing till six am
I chart a course through *Songs of Leonard Cohen*
watching the window in the door
turning my iPod wheel like a little helm
and lie down with *The Sisters*, and *Suzanne*
and find the lines for grief, the lines for shame
and taste the small rain falling from my cheek
and breathe the thin stars rising through my lungs.

Unsent SMS

Send a car. Send money. Send my cards back.
Send ███████ / Today wasn't as bad. I love
you / I need you but maybe you don't need me
anymore, my kind of broken baby-mother / I
know we fought today but ███████ / I don't
like it ████. The security lanyards and the
curtained beds, the way my room-mate looks at
me / Sort it out, my DEAR ███████ / I tell
the nurses about When I Still Lived at Home,
how we used to do his bath time
███████████ / You'll never know what it's
like to lose your ███████ / Have you talked to
Dr Stewart yet? / Just get me home / FFS / The
sun sets through the keyhole. Again. ███████

They don't warn you about the good bits:

blagging your way to the top of the tower-blocks,
leaves overtaking the estate, the seagulls
choreographed above the tree-line,
each tiny human brow anointed with kindness.

Nor your hands warm for healing touch,
the full-ripe joy, the completeness.

They don't tell you
how you will open a book to hear it read itself,
in a harmonic voice with the print
lifting from the pages, almost in dance.
No-one warns you of the beauty.

They don't tell you of the quests:
biscuit tin as weighty as a chalice,
life become fable. Nor the elation
as you lie in the hospital gym, certain
that with the next stretch you can fly.

Lauren squishing her ear into a CD
to have a listen,
Amber running from invisible bees
in gasping fits,
Lisa with her knickers in her hand again.

Mind you no one tells you either
of how they drag her down the corridor
by her clothing, inject her in the buttocks,
and how you are made
to collude in it, made witness.

Nor how afterwards you rise from your bed
and open your eyes to speak.

Voice of the fire setter

All childhood we played Ships and Lighthouses,
sailing near to the fire behind its mesh:
faces tinted orange by the ghost-soft flames.

It was Elijah's chariot we turned to
over and over in our Usborne Bible
and matchsticks were a weekly treat:

ten counted into cross-legged laps
like sweeties. I could smell the smoke
the moment they got me on the ward.

The cardamom warmth of the hearth
was back in my eyes, comforting and gritty.
We needed a burning, burning,

a cleansing of the hospital
like someone sterilising surgical instruments
– there were just too many of us sick.

Blistered against the spark wheel
my thumb teased out a tea-light flame,
let it die and called it forth again.

The thought of all those branching corridors
aflame from my little lighter, was as giddying
as an oak packed into an acorn.

Snow globe

Those weeks the summer waited for me like a snow globe,
around the time I thought I could fly, one of those weeks
when I felt elated by the glitter in the floor tiles
and my heart and mouth were full of song,

feet starry from the seeds and grains, the dust of noon
I was making and remaking the bed twice a day
half lifted on dry flaring storms
but he came only once, upturned my cloistered world.

The nurse said it wasn't my fault.
Evening dust played in the window
while I handed round parsley like Ophelia,
thinking she meant the sheets.

In sickness and in health

In a certain way   it barely matters
what was meds, what was illness:
but I went elsewhere   catatonic
shedding deadweight burdens
   for him to try and heave.

When my wedding band snapped
         it made a fault-line we dared not glimpse or cross
since which we have been gentle with one another.

Love became my adopted homeland.
Morning by morning I stand at the altar
pledging *I do, I do, I do.*

Selkie mother

Heart

Winter is the time her heart seeks to wander, wrung out and leaden, drawn with cramps, though she does everything she can to stop it. She tries to tether it with deliveries and concert dates but still it wants to stray. Every morning she beaches at 5:15, unprepared and empty-handed, nothing sifted, nothing darned. Winter is the time it would sever itself, float off. She pads about the house in the matted dark. Her heart still longs to snip its ties to her.

Womb

Her son had slipped out with the membrane over his scalp. Her womb had stayed behind, an old church, and a church ought not have weather but this one held ice between its panes, drips in its rafters, buckets at the end of each pew. She watched his small lungs inhale the amnion, eyes brimming over with salt. At least he would never drown.

Skin

It nestles at the back of the airing cupboard, pressed between tissue like a christening gown. Why would her husband not expect her to find it there? It still fits fine, even after pregnancy. The short fur has turned a little clumpy, yellow, tin and grey. All she needs do is roll it into her bag, run down the damp brown sand, pull the hood over like the baby's caul. The waves rising over and beneath her.

Abilify 15mg: half a tablet daily

The lunar phase identical each evening
perpetual half-moon
*

Light spilt from an Anglepoise lamp
the feel of corn-starch on the finger
*

Engine oil that overfills its tank
flooding the whole workings
*

Adhesive of my waking-sleeping mind
sealed tight against fantasia
*

A wafer on the tongue, dissolving
into insight or shame
*

The garlic clove of wellness, buried deep
in black soil like half a thumping heart

The music stops and my chair is gone

and every day now I'm clipboarding
electric toothbrushes, air con units,

tallying locusts, frogs, the death of firstborns,
the drizzle through the light-fitting,

dour angels holding back the four winds,
flames on the road to work, the end of days.

What happens if we don't pray? What if we do?
I blame myself so much. A paper above the bed

reads *Sectioned:* say it isn't so
and I will bind my head and stopper my ears

and feel again for the music, the chair, the children.

Crista

Like the twin I never had, you came
calling unannounced, wheeling your bike
the differences between us slight –
China for Lebanon; making art, not poetry.
After the first year a train undid you;
my husband forbidden to see
the mosaic.
The second year I crossed an unmarked, unfenced railway track
in front of the unannounced 10:17
and later that morning forgot the existence of my baby –
trailing scarves
– a rainbow in a doctors' bag –
to the psychiatric hospital
where the windows look out on indoors,
the doors (all locked) on bars and fences.
My indigo shawl: fractured wings.

After the stigmata, it took the first week to have breakfast
the second to find my programme
the third week was packing, packing
and in the fourth, I wrote.
Finally broken – as a horse is broken in –
undignified.

God enjoyeth that He is our moder

On the Unit they teach you how to play with your children
with gaudy playmats and hand-sized drums
with jack in the boxes and ukuleles –
they play with the children for you.
It is humiliation, it makes you humble.

And I couldn't play with him, and I didn't want to
so the nursery nurses showed me how
with smiles that had no understanding
of my numbness, my good-as-death numbness.

In Mother Julian's cell were three stone windows:
for bread, for teaching, for prayer.
Her breath misted out above the bricked-in
deathbed that God had visited.
It streamed on into the cold empty church.

My room on the Mother and Baby Unit was spacious,
thoughtfully furnished, wooden and clean
with a curtain in the door.
I too closed in on death but danced away,
fevered, feeling the cursor of consciousness
pass through my skull to wander the wards untethered.

And I have seen how prayer is answered
quietly, instinctively, without a fuss
like a mother's flannel on your burning forehead
while you turn and sleep on.

And I have felt a comfort close to me, to us,
holding my child nearer than the heart in my chest;
O pray for us still, Mother Julian –
al shal be wel, and al shal be wel, and
al manner of thyng shal be wele.

Metamorphosis

Nervous breakdown sounds a little soft
for my liking, just as *cocoon*
and *chrysalis* are too aerial
speaking nothing of the hard-shelled body bag
inside which a being privately disintegrates
privately rebuilds.

Discharge day

was the calm after a pneumatic drill
but they needed one last bloods

that no-one could coerce
from my tender veins.

All morning, the weather close,
shepherded from building to building,

I clutched my meds like a party bag:
Olanzapine, Diazepam.

I might have risen out of my own husk:
nebulous, just twenty-one grams, the soul's weight,

while happiness was scribbling away
in white ink about my future.

Definition of hope

Verb with infinitive: intend, if possible:
'she hoped to be heard'; 'he hoped to raise the child'.
Verb intrans: to want something to happen:
'they hoped for a long remission, perhaps till death.'
Count noun: 'his last hopes the tiny magic
of pills or seeds'. *Mass noun:* 'the hope we feel
as the butterfly crawls out, its wings still budded and moist';
Archaic: absolute trust. *Antonym:* nothing.

Say that my illness were a fairy child

and that for years I carried her unwittingly
but when the pangs came for him
she slipped out too, like a seal pup.
Say I blew raspberries into her belly button,
applying balms with cotton wool,
cradled her in lullabies and crochet,
lip-traced her non-existent eyebrows
and held out my pinkies to both small fists.

Well what else could I have done? Let's say it was love,
that I didn't care that my hair was disheveled.
and I wasn't prepared to be ashamed
of this colicky fey little changeling.
My daughter's my daughter for all of her life
– what was there to do but embrace her?

The friendship prescription

After wandering around A&E,
before falling into a grand mal seizure,
I prescribed myself *somebody to listen*.

In the absence of campfire and blankets
someone would huddle inside the tent of curtains
perch on my rickety metal bed.

And though this wasn't part of the hospital offering
since then I have been listened to, held
till there's no more *them* but all *us*,

a crocheted blanket around taut shoulders,
lips to the babies' warm fontanelles,
the white moon shifting on its anchor.

Hospital time

But it can't be psychosis if all of us
hear the recorder play itself upstairs
and see the blood and the muffled fire in the writing paper
of that ramshackle house, where Dad rises
at 3am to fix us stroganoff and we all of us
lie on the same bare mattress
watching a crucifix languidly spin.

It's just that we are more permeable before we dream
– like all the voices on the bus
or a radio tuned in to two channels at once –
which means it's okay to talk to Anna, who's dead.
Then I call for my meds and you tell me I've had them,
all of them, an hour ago. And that once again
it's hospital time. From upstairs, the tune of *London Bridge*.

The healing

I'd hoped to ease my shame with crab apple flower essence
though I'd never learned the dictionary of leaf and seed.

I'd staggered round wearily, baby in sling, to a neighbour
with the trees, plucking their heads into magenta Tupperware,

wanting all the stiffly cupped petals to float, infusing
with water and sun to an essence of the sacred Whole.

The Integrated Medicine Encyclopedia said *boil immediately*
but the baby started up like an outboard motor

until I leaned over the hump of him, pouring everything out,
the cream petals wavering in the grille of the drain.

Houses

They interviewed a guy on *Anglia*, the end wall
of his terrace blown clean off like a doll's house
                           and all the rooms visible.
Gym equipment, clothes rails, computer desk, twin divans.
He wasn't rich. Tumble dryer they said.
                           That's how my head feels –
like there's a hole instead of a staircase in the bedroom floor
like you can peer down through the sitting room ceiling
by hanging over the bed, giddy and vertiginous
or like you might light up all the water in the pipes with potassium
screaming at dog-whistle pitch that you want to go home.

Some of them – some of us – kill our babies.
We drive cars into walls or walk off bridges.
I want to kiss those women on their foreheads and say
you're not bad you're not bad I see you and you're not a bad person

and fasten all the doors on their broken dolls' houses.

Cottage garden

When I imagine
Dr Bach at Mount Vernon,
his cup and saucer still lukewarm
he is barefoot or leather-sandaled
among the dew and hollyhocks,
stooping to finger each bud,
and I want to believe, too, that God has touched
the antidote for each distress
into the flowers.

When I was at my worst
gulping Rescue Remedy
couldn't help me. Nothing could.
But now, clematis brings me down to earth.
Clematis, which he recommends
for those *not fully awake*.
I think I believe in this.
(Old English *belyfan*. Literally, *to love*.)

Family planning (ii)

Coil fitting

If it happened again,
it would just about finish me off:
the nights, the years before they speak,
the not knowing what their cries mean;
the waiting for all the souls
of all my dead
to come back as babies
in prams in corridors
every wedding ring,
name and generation
flaming into one.

The nurse strips away the packaging:
little copper T-bar
an anchor to wedge
in the seabed of my body.
I cough
when she asks me to
and almost smile
as my womb clamps down
though the pain
is sunset-coloured and cloudy
a claret spasm
which makes me think
of miscarriage
the seahorse on a towel
in the bathroom
and I will bear this too, I will bear it

my fingers feeling for small threads
of reassurance.

James and the catkins

I was sickening for psychosis, more than sickening
and you were less than two, just starting to talk
and I made a game for you as we walked the woodland path
putting all the catkins into houses under leaves.
You tottered about, repeating *'pillar, home.*
Sometimes that is all any of us need, a place to be our home.
You took all of your babies and laid them to sleep.
I used to invent innocent games for you
and when I was ill and I knew I wasn't thinking straight
I begged my mother to hold you, to keep you safe
like her arms were my arms loving you.
I knew I shouldn't hold you.
I knew.

The NHS is no place for witchery

but to raise up a candle or sachet
the heartfelt murmur of prayer or incantation
is an intuitive fumbling after wellness.

I have hidden spikenard essential oil in a real glass vial
up my dressing-gown sleeve
to anoint the bathwater with blurry dots.

Tides of lavender shift beneath the waterline
where bees murmur, and a censer swings its scent
slow and mauve and majestic.

And when my chaperone's eyes turn matte as sea gems
the long, thin room is a meadow in Provence
and if I could but stay there, only stay.

Milk-tooth

I blindly pat the mattress to claim your first tooth
till one fingertip catches
on a hollow root tapering to bluntness
so big in your mouth, so small on my palm.
Built with mother's milk, Calpol syringes
and soggy muslins.

Oh tears and blood, oh unbridged gap,
oh implacable loss, never to be returned.
My milk is gone now and my hair is grey
I have wrapped the incisor in tissue
in a keepsake box with your hospital nametag
and the quilted elephant blanket
and the other tag, from our other stay,
the one you don't know about.

Landskein

The hut tilted and in came the tide, gathering jars and books from my shelves – but it was their time. Through the bobbing window there was still that one dark stain between sea and sky, the inky line spreading into the water and into the wind, and I was no longer distinct but every thing, water and sky and hut, and poised to carry myself on the currents over the threshold and onto the beach. Carry myself I did, tenderly as a coffin, over pebbles and sea-worn debris and then I turned onto my back and soared out over the expanse and my hair was free, my hair was the clouds and then the clouds all gone. Birds patterned and re-patterned overhead: gulls, cormorants. Brine and boat-paint turned a single fragrance in the lungs, and the movement of the waves, and what remained of me, were travelling on the air. I was a box-kite, filled and steadily wavering, my voice coarse as a gull's, the gathering sky darker than the beach, its smear of sunset sharp. In the sea's deep pulse, a reconciliation with all those hearts I hadn't understood. Then a brace of strong arms hoisted me: *you can let go now.*

Snowstorm

Paper doll in an upturned jam jar,
waiting for the flakes to settle
so that she can see.

Snow scene

Children are scurrying underfoot through the
house, and our troubles are all but forgotten, and
Dad's about to carve, and there's the scent of
wine, and frying onions, and sweet cinnamon or
maybe it's a little later, carols over, washing up
dealt with and if this were a film we might almost
patter out onto the street and you'd jump on my
hip, legs asunder, though you're big now, your
thighs long and colt-like, nothing left of toddler
softness and we'd spin, our heads back, eyeing
the roofs and the deep clouds, one white streak
of moon wavering and the sky bobbing with stars
and the leaves of snow turning and slowly
floating down and you'd urge me to *make a wish,*
and I'd kiss your forehead – and then it's the music.

Homecoming

Every few weeks something draws me back
and then it's the first daffs bobbing on thin stems
or the sun canoodling bricks again
or a windowful of stars.
Later months, I feel it watch over me –
coasting down green-lined avenues
or making a den of faded sheets
or dancing with livid abandon.

Sometimes, it's the low beams streaming the allotments
and warming the planks of our new treehouse
or plaiting white netting round a kayak
in the last hours of a Sunday evening
when just for a moment, anxiety loosens
and I sense it through the paddle and I know.

Intercession

O Mother Julian, you had the
good sense to invite your
sickness, mine snuck up on
me. You shared Christ-visions,
your rood and your hazelnut,
I dreamt with eyes open; all
incense and parsley-leaf, etching
fire symbols onto the night sky.
You chose the walls of your
anchor-hold, but I had my own
confinement. Your Goddess is
a mother continuously carrying
us. In her womb we are remade:
our lives knit together from
frayed odds and ends. I have
never seen who it was made me.
I light this candle in the name
of my child, salvaged by love.
The walls will not hold. Please
Mother pray for us.

How to do your needlework

i

Cut out fragments of old baby-grows, feeding cloths;
arrange the fabrics, colour match carefully.

The midwife called my body *a jigsaw*
and the sutures she made unraveled.

ii

Press your blocks onto paper, pin and keep safe
between sheets of parchment like old flowers.

I piece together the scraps in my head,
the imagined golden thread. The aftermath.

iii

Arrange top sides together
with steel thimble, a fine and extra-long needle.

Everything carried too much significance,
publishers' addresses or the brands of soap.

iv

Start at the borders, work towards the centre-point.

Had they brought him to me
those nights I lay almost anaesthetised
I might still have breastfed.

v

Meandering stitches on the quilt top,
but stab stitch through the deep layers.

I save and press the frayed ends,
some of it hurting me.

vi

Each row of sewing should be neat hyphens
as if to indicate missing text.

(where I nuzzled - - - dense on my left side
where they wouldn't let - - keep needles).

vii

To birth the quilt: sew along three sides,
turn right way out.

When I had him, I lost the thread,
my mind left half inside the womb.

viii

Label the underside with Baby's name, yours, the year.

James, son of Jenny, 2013.
The hospital fabric looks prettier now, as if
a clearwing moth should stretch down her legs to bless

The Book of Thank You

I cupped my hands,
the petals fell into them,
lightly.
I opened my lips,
a tune emerged
like a freed wren.
It was warm in the park
and the magnolias
were candelabra.

Acknowledgements and Thanks

The publications in which some of these poems first appeared:

'Definition of Love', 'Night crossing' (i) and (ii), 'Boy of Jenny Pagdin', 'Insanity', 'What to pack for the Caldbeck Mother & Baby Unit', 'Crista', 'Metamorphosis', 'Definition of hope', 'Cottage garden' and 'On Whom the Rain Comes Down' were first published in my Eyewear pamphlet *Caldbeck* (2017). 'Not tawny, never brass' appeared in the *Spoonfeed* blog 2023. *Ink, Sweat & Tears* published 'On Whom the Rain Comes Down' – May 2018 and 'The Book of Thank You' – May 2021. *Interpreter's House* published 'Intercession' in 2023. *Smoke Magazine* 67 published 'Newborn' – 2021. *Wild Court* published 'James and the catkins' (under a previous title) – 2020 and 'Landskein' – 2022. *New Welsh Review* published 'Say that my illness were a fairy child' – 2021. *Ambit* published 'The healing' – 2021, and 'Voice of the fire setter', 'Discharge day' and 'Hospital time' – 2022. *The Mum Poem Press Songs of Love and Strength Anthology* includes 'Milk tooth', 2021. 'Gore' appeared on the Café Writers website after winning second prize in their 2021 competition, as did 'Houses' (Commended). 'Ursa Major' was first published as part of the 2023 Bridport Prize Anthology, having been Highly Commended in the competition. Additionally, 'How to do your needlework' was shortlisted for the 2023 Bridport Prize.

My thanks and gratitude to the following people:

My family, who have allowed me the time and freedom to write.

Jane Commane and Nine Arches Press for the wonderful editorial and caring support throughout the generation of *The Snow Globe*.

My mentor Liz Berry for giving me the keys to these poems, and for unfailing encouragement and warmth.

The late Avril Bruten, who first encouraged me about my writing.

Eyewear/Black Spring Press Group and particularly Todd Swift and Rosanna Hildyard for first publishing versions of many of these poems in my pamphlet *Caldbeck*.

Rebecca Goss for her support and encouragement with some of these poems.

Julia Webb and the Norwich Stanza for their astute readings and suggestions, and for the friendships.

The Creative Writing faculty at University of East Anglia, particularly George Szirtes.

Sarah Westcott, Caroline Bird, Denise Riley, Michael Flexer, Kevin McAleer, Peggy Hughes, and Kim Moore, for encouragement along the way.

Action on Postpartum Psychosis for their unfailing support.

Postpartum Psychosis

Postpartum Psychosis (PP) is a severe, but treatable, form of mental illness that occurs after having a baby. It can happen 'out of the blue' to women without previous experience of mental illness. There are some groups of women, women with a history of bipolar disorder for example, who are at much higher risk. PP normally begins in the first few days to weeks after childbirth. It can get worse very quickly and should always be treated as a medical emergency. Most women need to be treated with medication and admitted to hospital.

With the right treatment, women with PP do make a full recovery. Recovery takes time and the journey may be tough. The illness can be frightening and shocking for both the woman experiencing it and her family. Women do return to their normal selves, and are able to regain the mothering role they expected. There is no evidence that the baby's long term development is affected by Postpartum Psychosis.

Action on Postpartum Psychosis
https://www.app-network.org